WORLD'S SCARIEST PLACES

GHOSTLY PRISONS

ALIX WOOD

Gareth Stevens PUBLISHING

Please visit our website, **www.garethstevens.com**. For a free color catalog of all our high-quality books, call toll free 1-800-542-2595 or fax 1-877-542-2596

Cataloging-in-Publication Data
Names: Wood, Alix.
Title: Ghostly prisons / Alix Wood.
Description: New York : Gareth Stevens, 2017. | Series: World's scariest places | Includes index.
Identifiers: ISBN 9781482459043 (pbk.) | ISBN 9781482459067 (library bound) |
ISBN 9781482459050 (6 pack)
Subjects: LCSH: Haunted prisons--Juvenile literature. | Ghosts--Juvenile literature.
Classification: LCC BF1477.3 W66 2017 | DDC 133.1'22--dc23

First Edition

Published in 2017 by
Gareth Stevens Publishing
111 East 14th Street, Suite 349
New York, NY 10003

Produced for Gareth Stevens by Alix Wood Books
Designed by Alix Wood
Editor: Eloise Macgregor

Photo credits: Cover, 1, 27 top © Miranda Wood; 4, 6, 12 right, 25 top © AdobeStock; 5 top © C.C. Chapman; 5 bottom © Carl Cutland; 7 top © Barbara Champlin; 7 bottom © Royal Holloway Collection; 8 © Al Girdas; 9 top © Yves Bernicot; 9 bottom © Pegasoreise; 10 © Jim McIntosh; 11 top © Richard Moross; 11 bottom © Christian Haugen; 12 left © Carcea Daniel; 13 © Albert Dobrin; 14 main © Anthony J; 14 inset © Army Museum; 15 © M. K. Feeney; 16 © Velvet; 17 top © Ralf Peter Reimann; 17 bottom © Jeanette Warner; 18, 25 bottom, 29 bottom © Shutterstock; 19 top © Crisco; 19 bottom © Karen; 20 © Australian War Memorial; 21 © Maki Lika; 22 © Dore Vabelfiore; 23 top © T. Hesab; 23 bottom © H. Rae; 24 © Bjoert Vedt; 26-27 © Ed Lynch-Bell; 28 © Edward Stojakovic; 29 top © Spencer Cross

Printed in China

CPSIA compliance information: Batch #CW17GS. For further information contact Gareth Stevens, New York, New York at 1-800-542-2595.

Contents

Most people would probably agree that prisons are pretty unpleasant places, even if you don't believe in ghosts. Imagine how much scarier a jail would be if it was actually haunted!

A ghost is believed to be the spirit of a dead person. Ghosts are thought to haunt places where terrible things have happened. Prisons certainly fit that description!

Prisons can be full of very scary people. You would think ghosts wouldn't want to stay there either! But some old prisoners seem very reluctant to leave.

IT'S EASY TO GET SPOOKED IN A CASTLE DUNGEON!

Wicklow Gaol (jail) in Ireland is known as "The Gates of Hell" because of the many ghost sightings there! A member of staff was once pushed out of the gates (left) by an unseen force!

Spooky mists have been seen floating around the second floor walkway. Story has it a little girl haunts the schoolroom, and the ghost of a prison **matron** has been seen, too!

The Tower of London, England

The Tower of London was built around 1100, designed to terrify any unruly people living in sight of it. It was used to imprison, **torture**, or **execute** anyone who caused problems to the King. Prisoners were brought to the Tower by boat after their trial. The executioner stood behind them on the boat, and pointed his ax toward the prisoner if he was to be put to death. Crowds would then know to gather for a public execution! Queen Anne Boleyn, Lady Jane Grey, and many others met their death at the Tower, and are now said to haunt it.

Bears were once kept at the Tower. A guard is believed to have dropped dead from shock after seeing a ghostly bear there!

Queen Anne Boleyn was married to King Henry VIII. She was arrested, and beheaded on Tower Green in 1536. Only "friends of the King" were executed there as it was more private than Tower Hill! Legend has it her ghost has been seen on the Green and in the chapel. People even say her headless body walks through the Tower's corridors!

Two young princes were imprisoned and murdered in the Tower. Poeple often claim the ghosts of the two boys are often seen at the Tower. They are usually wearing their nightgowns, holding hands, and looking terrified. In 1674, two small skeletons were found buried beneath a stone staircase! In 1993, the skeletons were examined and found to belong to two boys, who would have been around ten and twelve years old.

Karosta Prison, Latvia

No one has ever escaped from Karosta, a former **Soviet** military prison. Hundreds of prisoners died at the site, many of whom were shot by the **Nazis** for being **deserters**. The prison only closed in 1997. There have been many strange ghostly happenings at the prison. The ghost of a woman known as the "White Lady" wanders the hallways looking for her future husband. She hung herself after visiting her fiancé held prisoner there, only to be told he had already been executed.

The prison is now a quirky hotel! Visitors can enjoy a "prisoner experience" at Karosta. Guests are shouted at, made to exercise, and sleep on the floor in the haunted cells!

Brave visitors to Karosta prison have experienced cell doors creaking and seen strange shadows moving around the building. Some have heard footsteps and whispered warnings, or felt as if they were being touched or tugged at.

Tuol Sleng, Cambodia

Between 1975 and 1979 this former high school was taken over by the **Khmer Rouge** and used as a prison. It was one of the most brutal places the world has ever seen. Prisoners were tortured into confessing they were an enemy of the Khmer Rouge. They were then made to name other enemies of the regime, who were also captured, tortured, and killed.

It is thought that almost everyone killed at Tuol Sleng was innocent. Around 17,000 men, women, and children were imprisoned there, and only seven people are known to have survived.

THE PRISON AT TUOL SLENG IS NOW A MUSEUM.

A TORTURE ROOM AT TUOL SLENG

Staff at the museum are now trying to identify photographs taken of the thousands of victims. They believe ghosts appear in the room with them as they work. Unseen hands have been heard leafing through the photos and records! The workers think that the ghosts are trying to help them. At lunch, staff leave food out for the ghosts. They appear starving, and will often go away once they have been given food.

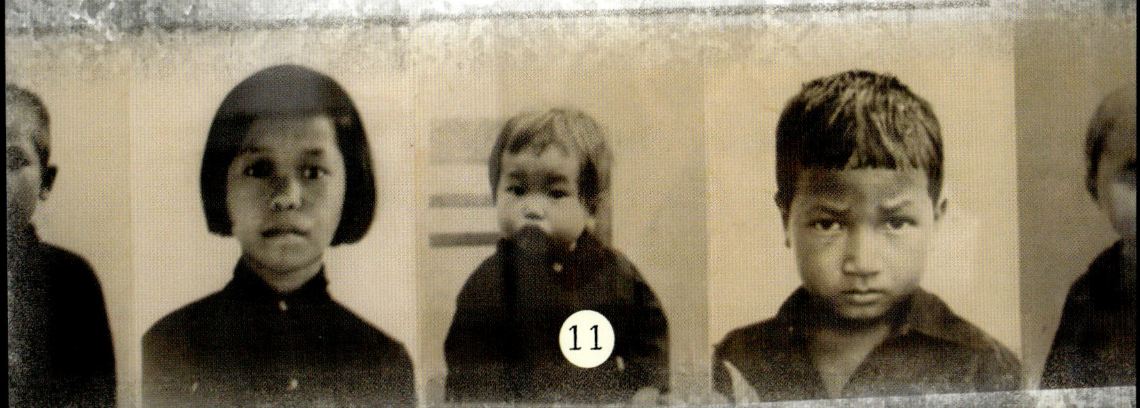

Corvin Castle, Transylvania

This spooky castle certainly looks as if it is straight out of a horror movie! Bloodthirsty **tyrant** Vlad the Impaler was once kept prisoner at Corvin Castle. Vlad was a prince and a member of the House of Dracula. He inspired the author Bram Stoker's story about the **vampire**, Count Dracula. This may explain the vampire-like ghosts that have been seen wandering the corridors!

VLAD THE IMPALER WAS IMPRISONED IN THE CASTLE.

Some tourists tricked the guards and stayed overnight at the castle. They came out bruised and terrified, saying they had been attacked by an angry ghost!

In one of the towers, a small **niche** was built. A priest would hide there and spy on conversations in the dining room between the **nobles**. He would then tell the master of the house if any of them were plotting against him or the king. Finally, legend says, one priest was caught spying, and the angry nobles walled him inside the niche alive! Perhaps he is responsible for some of the haunting of the castle? Some visitors have seen ghostly silhouettes appear in photographs they have taken at the castle.

The Halifax Citadel, Canada

This star-shaped fort is almost 300 years old. The Citadel is said to be home to several ghosts. In the Cavalier Building, below, a gray woman in Victorian clothes who smells of roses has been seen rocking in a rocking chair on the balcony. She may have been a sergeant's wife believed to have died in a fire there in 1889. Some say she may be a bride-to-be whose fiancé killed himself right before the wedding.

THE CAVALIER BUILDING

The Cavalier Building in the parade square was used as a prisoner of war camp during World War I. The prisoners were mainly Germans living in Canada at the time.

The garrison cells (right) housed soldiers being punished for minor crimes. The prisoners slept on iron cots with nothing to do but stare at the walls. The area is now haunted. A visitor claimed the ghost of a soldier walked into a room and then vanished!

The two wells that once supplied the Citadel with water are both boarded up. One was full of rats. The other is said to contain the remains of a sergeant! He fell down the well, and some of his body was recovered, but no one wanted to drink from the well after that. People say the sergeant is still occasionally seen walking the grounds.

During the ghost tours that take place at the Citadel, a small girl is said to follow the groups, and will sometimes hold people's hands!

Kilmainham Gaol, Ireland

The old prison in Kilmainham, Dublin, was built in 1796. The conditions at the gaol, or jail, were appalling. Men, women, and children were often held together in packed cells. The youngest child imprisoned there was just seven years old! Years later, leaders of the 1916 **Easter Rising** were imprisoned and executed there by the British. The jail is believed to be haunted. Many prison guards would ask to be transferred to another jail, because of the strange, ghostly atmosphere there.

Kilmainham Gaol closed in 1924. Many believe it closed because the hauntings became too disruptive. Prisoners were sometimes said to be let out of their cells by invisible forces!

KILMAINHAM GAOL

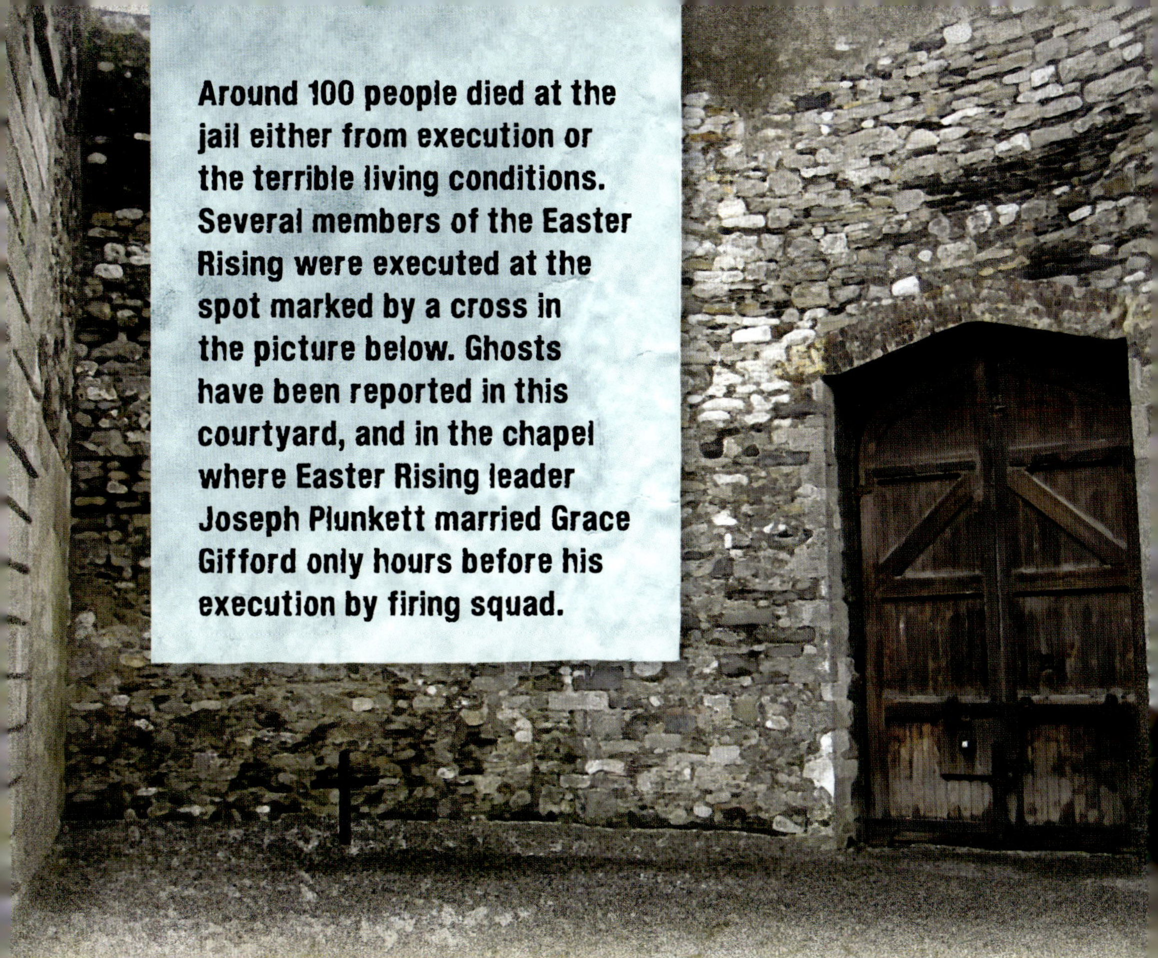

Around 100 people died at the jail either from execution or the terrible living conditions. Several members of the Easter Rising were executed at the spot marked by a cross in the picture below. Ghosts have been reported in this courtyard, and in the chapel where Easter Rising leader Joseph Plunkett married Grace Gifford only hours before his execution by firing squad.

PRISONERS WERE HUNG FROM BEAMS THAT USED TO STICK OUT FROM THESE HOLES ABOVE THE ENTRANCE.

During the jail's restoration, workers saw lights mysteriously turning on, and heard ghostly footsteps. One scared man fled to the chapel where he was thrown across the room and then lifted off the ground by an invisible force!

Lawang Sewu, Indonesia

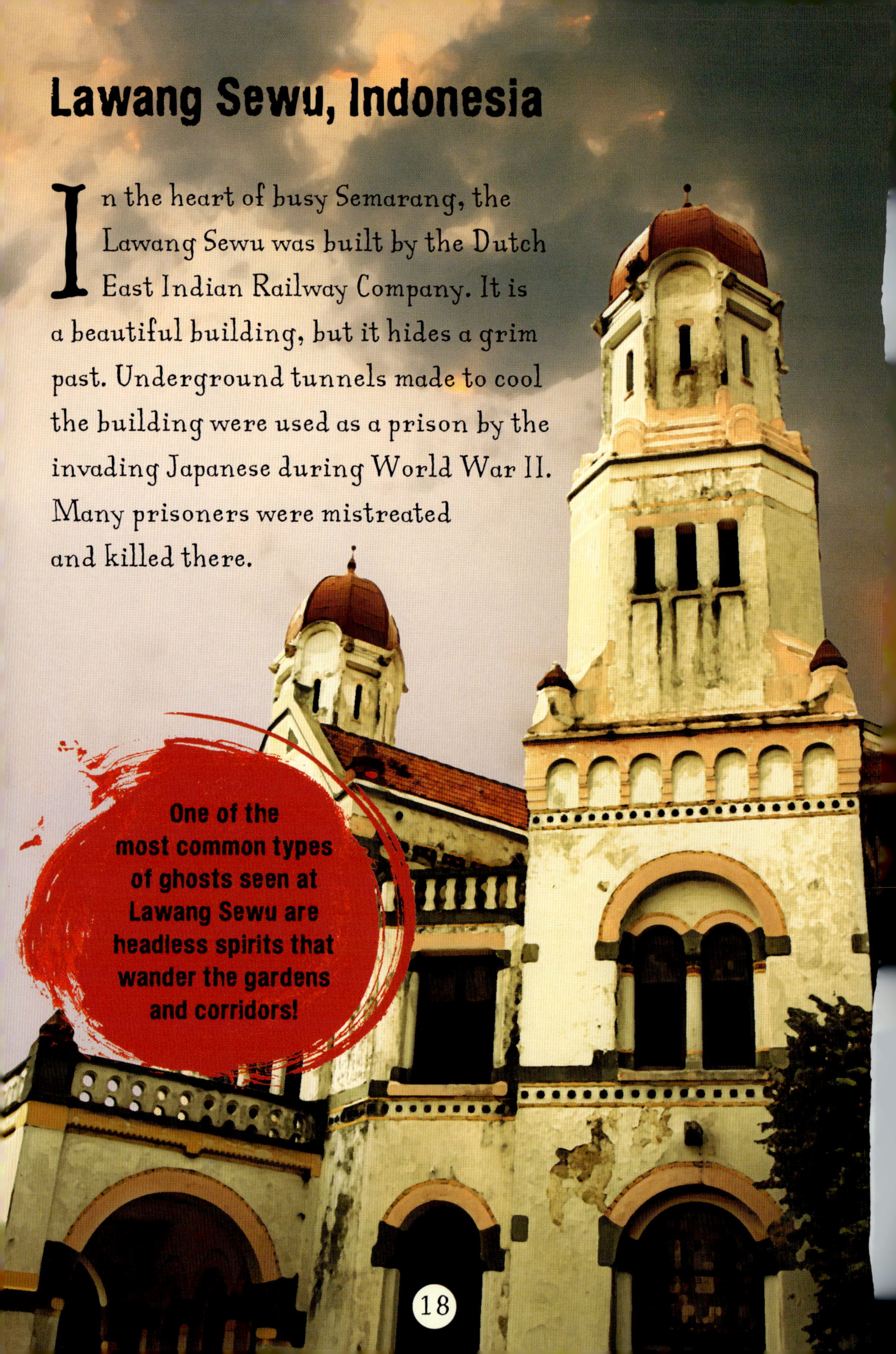

In the heart of busy Semarang, the Lawang Sewu was built by the Dutch East Indian Railway Company. It is a beautiful building, but it hides a grim past. Underground tunnels made to cool the building were used as a prison by the invading Japanese during World War II. Many prisoners were mistreated and killed there.

One of the most common types of ghosts seen at Lawang Sewu are headless spirits that wander the gardens and corridors!

Lawang Sewu's basement prison area is the spookiest. A Dutch woman is believed to have killed herself there and she haunts the area. Her ghost was apparently caught on camera during the filming of an Indonesian ghost hunter TV program!

A creepy spiral staircase leads up to the attic of one of the towers. People have experienced feeling a woman brush past them on the stairs. She is said to have long hair and a bloodied face.

The Death Railway, Thailand

Some prisons may not have four walls and iron bars. **Allied** prisoners of war during World War II were forced by their Japanese captors to build the Burma Railway. They worked in terrible conditions to build the difficult rail link between Bangkok in Thailand and Burma (now known as Myanmar). Around 90,000 Southeast Asian laborers and 12,621 Allied prisoners died during the construction. The Allies were mainly British, Australian, Dutch, and American.

A man is said to have died for every sleeper laid along the 250-mile (402 km) railway.

AUSTRALIAN PRISONERS CARRYING RAILWAY SLEEPERS

The surviving section of the route is now a popular train journey for visitors. The train hangs onto the steep cliffs and crosses the river over wooden bridges. The journey is not an amusement park ride, however. Visitors speak of experiencing an overwhelming feeling of sorrow and a ghostly atmosphere, heavy with the spirits of so many dead.

Camps housing workers were built every few miles along the route. Trying to escape was pointless. The thick jungle, language problems, and the lack of maps, food, or medicine made escape difficult. Large sums of money were given to anyone who captured an escaped prisoner, too. The Japanese threatened terrible punishments on people left in the camps if anyone escaped.

THE RAILWAY HUGGING A CLIFF FACE

Eastern State Penitentiary, Pennsylvania

Bad guys such as gangster Al Capone and bank robber Willie Sutton were held at ESP, as it was known. By the 1940s, staff and prisoners started saying they had seen ghostly presences, or had eerie experiences in the old prison. In one of the guard towers, a shadowy figure has been seen keeping watch.

ESP has such a reputation for being haunted that they now run several ghost tours.

The ghost tour organizers ship in two scary gargoyles to sit over the entrance every fall, specially for the Halloween tours!

Al Capone managed to make his cell quite homey compared to everyone else's. He was haunted by a ghost in his cell, though. Inmates heard him screaming for Jimmy to leave him alone. He had murdered a man named James Clark, and it is believed it was his ghost haunting Capone.

AL CAPONE'S CELL

Visitors to the haunted prison have heard cries coming from the cells, and ghostly footsteps pacing the yard and the cells. In Cell Block 12 people have heard creepy laughter. A locksmith working in Cell Block 4 felt like someone was gripping him so tight he was unable to move! He also saw terrifying faces appear on the walls.

Akershus Castle, Norway

This medieval castle was built to protect Oslo, the capital of Norway. It has also been used as a prison. In the 1700s, the prison held minor criminals who were used as slaves. Many died of disease and the harsh conditions. During World War II, the Nazis used the castle to imprison Norwegian resistance fighters. Many were executed in the castle's courtyard.

Akershus Castle is believed to be the most haunted place in Norway. Story has it the ghost of a woman wearing a long robe has been seen wandering in the corridors. People who have seen her say that she has no face!

One of the scariest ghosts to haunt Akershus Castle is a dog named Malcanisen. Back when the castle was built it was a custom to bury a living animal by the front door! This was believed to protect the castle from intruders.

A dark passage in front of the original main entrance is haunted by the snarling dog. Soldiers were terrified if they saw it. Anyone who saw Malcanisen was said to suffer death soon after.

The ghost of a horse has also been heard by the old entrance. According to legend, a drunk Swedish soldier rode past the castle shouting that he would conquer Norway. Norwegian soldiers shot him and his horse, which now haunts the passageway.

Tiny, burning women, known as "nightpyres," are also believed to haunt the castle. They are said to have an ugly grin and a creepy laugh, and appear before any fires that have occurred at the castle.

Bodmin Jail, England

Bodmin Jail is an ancient prison on the edge of the desolate Bodmin Moor. The building is now a ruin, and also a tourist attraction. It was a bit of a tourist attraction when it was open, too. Hundreds of local people would gather to watch the many executions that took place at the jail!

Legend has it one ghost that haunts the jail is that of Anne Jefferies, believed to be a witch. The court at Bodmin demanded she was starved to death until she confessed to witchcraft. She never confessed, but it took three months for her to die. This made people more convinced she was a witch!

THE JAIL'S SPOOKY TOWER CAN BE SEEN ACROSS THE MOOR.

The Navy took over a wing of the jail to keep their prisoners. This crumbling area of the jail is said to be haunted by a thin man, believed to have been a naval prisoner. He may have starved to death. Stones are often thrown by invisible forces in this area, perhaps by him!

One of the creepiest ghosts is Selina Wadge, hanged for the murder of her young son. She is said to try to grab any children who visit the jail!

Matthew Weeks was hanged for his girlfriend's murder. His ghost is said to wander around the jail claiming his innocence. Children have been heard screaming in the basement cells. Many visitors experience the feeling of being watched, or touched.

Pottawatomie Jail, Iowa

Known as "The Squirrel Cage," Pottowatomie Jail had a very unusual cell design. Ten cells shaped like pieces of a pie formed a circle. The jail had three floors, and each floor had one door and ten cells. A hand crank would turn the cells. When the jailer needed a certain prisoner to leave their cell, they would crank the cells around until their cell door lined up with the door opening!

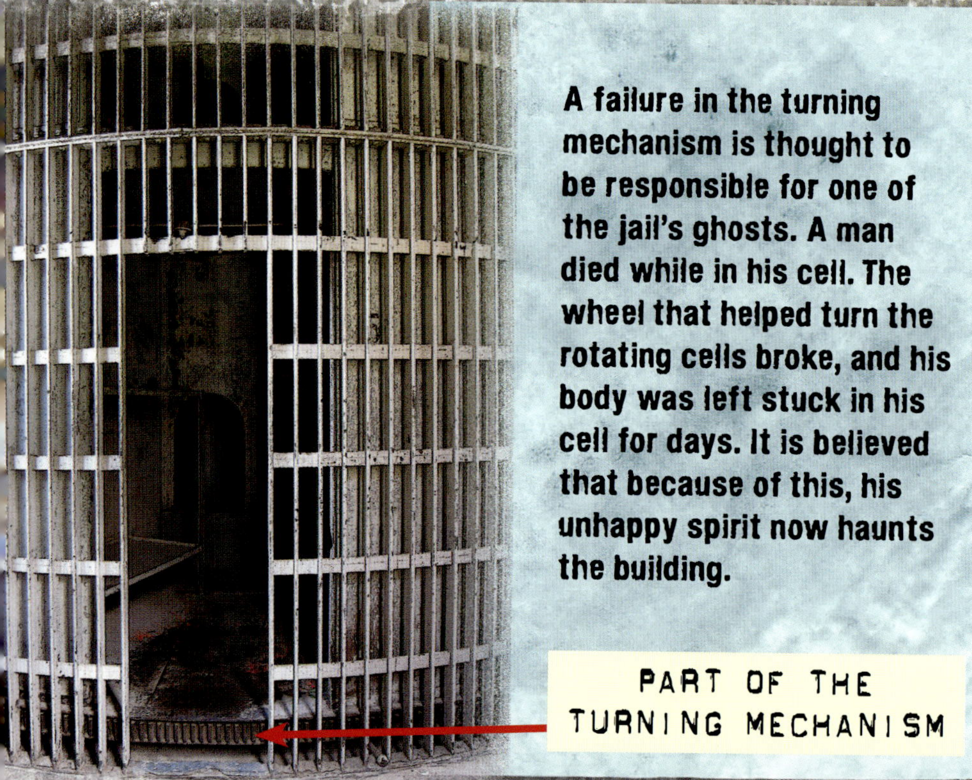

A failure in the turning mechanism is thought to be responsible for one of the jail's ghosts. A man died while in his cell. The wheel that helped turn the rotating cells broke, and his body was left stuck in his cell for days. It is believed that because of this, his unhappy spirit now haunts the building.

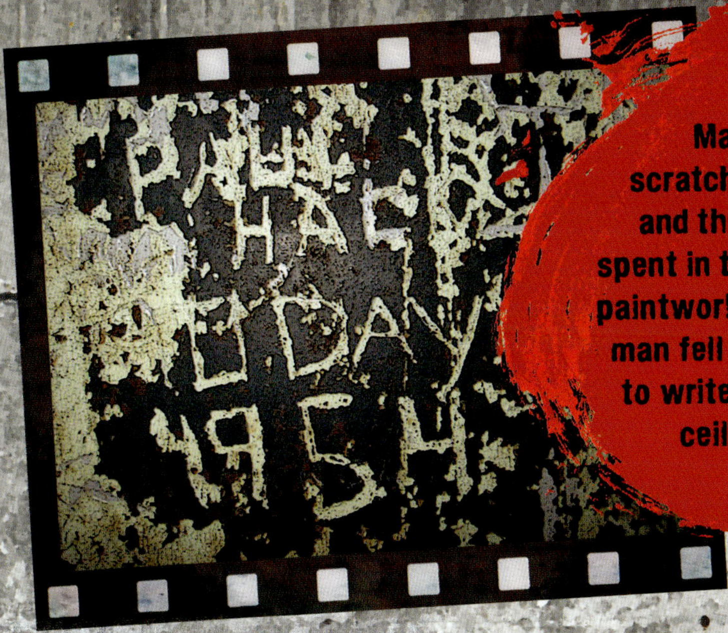

Many inmates scratched their names, and the time they had spent in their cells, into the paintwork. One unfortunate man fell while attempting to write his name on the ceiling and died!

It's not just prisoners that haunt this jail. Jailer J.M. Carter oversaw the building of the jail. He lived in the fourth floor apartment and, some believe, has never left! Another former jailer, Otto Gufath, also has been seen on the fourth floor. In the 1950s, jailer Bill Foster refused to live in the apartment. He would hear people walking on the fourth floor even though he knew it was empty. He decided to sleep on the second floor instead!

Glossary

Allied Relating to the nations united against Germany in World War I or World War II.

deserters Military personnel who quit their post without permission.

Easter Rising An armed rebellion in Dublin in 1916 against British rule in Ireland.

execute To put to death as a punishment.

gargoyle A waterspout in the form of a frightening human or animal figure.

Khmer Rouge A communist guerrilla organization that opposed the Cambodian government in the 1960s.

matron A woman who supervises women prisoners in a jail.

Nazis Members of a German fascist party controlling Germany from 1933 to 1945.

niche A hollowed-out place in a wall.

nobles A person of noble rank or birth.

Soviet People of the Union of Soviet Socialist Republics.

torture To punish or force someone to do or say something by causing great pain.

tyrant A person who uses authority or power harshly.

vampire A dead person believed to come from the grave at night and suck sleeping people's blood.

Further Information

Summers, Alex. *Haunted Prisons and Asylums (Yikes! It's Haunted)*. Vero Beach, FL: Rourke Publishing Group, 2016.

Williams, Dinah. *Haunted Prisons (Scary Places)*. New York, NY: Bearport Publishing, 2014.

Website

Facts for kids about the Tower of London:
primaryfacts.com/1343/15-tower-of-london-facts/

Publisher's note to educators and parents:
Our editors have carefully reviewed these websites to ensure that they are suitable for students. Many websites change frequently, however, and we cannot guarantee that a site's future contents will continue to meet our high standards of quality and educational value. Be advised that students should be closely supervised whenever they access the Internet.

Index

Don't be scared! Most people don't believe ghosts are real at all. No one has ever scientifically proven they exist. But it can be fun to get yourself a little spooked!